THE WARFARE OF BUSINESS

In this guide, we will be examining a list of 15 rules for a gunfight adapted from the US Military and exploring how they can be applied to the business world to make you and your organization more successful. These rules, which were developed through years of experience in high-stakes, high-pressure situations, provide valuable insights into the mindset and tactics needed to succeed in any competitive environment. By understanding and internalizing these principles, you will be better equipped to navigate the challenges and opportunities of the business world and achieve your goals. Whether you're a CEO, manager, or entry-level employee, these rules will help you to be more effective, efficient, and successful in your work.

DAN KNUDSON

The List

The 15 Rules for a Gunfight is a set of guidelines developed by the United States Marine Corps (USMC) for the use of firearms in combat. These rules were first introduced in the late 1980s as part of a larger effort to improve the USMC's tactics and training. The rules were designed to be simple and easy to remember, and to be applicable to a wide range of combat situations. They cover topics such as gun handling, target acquisition, and tactical movement, and are considered to be a fundamental part of the USMC's combat doctrine. The 15 Rules for a Gunfight are still in use today, and are taught to all Marines as part of their basic training. Overall it is a set of guidelines that focus on the proper handling and use of firearms in a combat situation and are aimed at increasing the chances of survival in a firefight.

1. Be courteous to everyone, friendly to no one.
2. Decide to be aggressive ENOUGH, quickly ENOUGH.
3. Have a plan.
4. Have a back-up plan, because the first one probably won't work.
5. Be polite. Be professional. But, have a plan to kill everyone you meet.
6. Do not attend a gunfight with a handgun whose caliber does not start with a "4."
7. Anything worth shooting is worth shooting twice. Ammo is cheap. Life is expensive.
8. Move away from your attacker. Distance is your friend. (Lateral and diagonal movement are preferred.)
9. Use cover or concealment as much as possible.
10. Flank your adversary when possible. Protect yours.
11. Always cheat; always win. The only unfair fight is the one you lose.
12. In ten years nobody will remember the details of caliber, stance, or tactics. They will only remember who lived.
13. If you are not shooting, you should be communicating or reloading.

14. Someday someone may kill you with your own gun, but they should have to beat you to death with it because it is empty.

15. And above all ... don't drop your guard.

CHAPTER 1: BE COURTEOUS TO EVERYONE, FRIENDLY TO NO ONE

It's not personal, it's just business." - Michael Corleone, The Godfather.

"Be courteous to everyone, friendly to no one" - In business, this means being professional and respectful with all colleagues and clients, while maintaining a level of distance and objectivity in order to make the best decisions.

In the fast-paced and competitive world of business, it is important to maintain a level of professionalism and respect with all colleagues and clients. However, it is also important to maintain a level of distance and objectivity in order to make the best decisions for the company or project. This is where the principle of "Be courteous to everyone, friendly to no one" comes in.

Being courteous means being respectful and polite in all interactions, whether it's with a client, a colleague, or a competitor. It means being punctual, attentive, and responsive to others' needs. It also means being honest and transparent in all communications.

Being friendly, on the other hand, can cloud judgment and lead to unproductive relationships. It's important to maintain a level of distance and objectivity in order to make the best decisions for the company or project. This doesn't mean being cold or aloof, but it does mean not becoming too close or too invested in personal relationships with colleagues or clients.

By following the principle of "Be courteous to everyone, friendly to no one," one can maintain a level of professionalism and respect while also keeping a clear head and making the best decisions for the company or project.

Business Rules as they apply to Rule 1:
1. Maintain professionalism: It's important to maintain a professional demeanor and treat all colleagues, clients and partners with respect, even if you don't agree with them or they are not your friends.
2. Maintain objectivity: It's important to maintain objectivity in your interactions with others and not let personal feelings or biases influence your decisions or actions.
3. Build a professional network: It's important to build a professional network and maintain positive relationships with people in your industry, even if you don't consider them friends.
4. Be aware of potential threats: It's important to be aware of potential threats, such as competitors, and take steps to protect yourself and your business.
5. Be strategic in your communication: It's important to be strategic in your communication and not reveal too much personal information or share confidential information with the wrong people.

Real World Application:
Imagine a situation where a large company is in the process of acquiring a smaller company. The acquisition is expected to bring significant benefits to the larger company, but it is also expected

to result in significant job losses and changes in the organizational structure of the smaller company.

As the acquisition process unfolds, the management team of the larger company will need to interact with a variety of stakeholders, including employees of the smaller company, shareholders, and regulatory authorities. In this scenario, it is important for the management team to maintain a professional demeanor and treat everyone with respect, even if they do not agree with them or if they are not on the same side of the issue. By being courteous and respectful to everyone, the management team can help to build trust and reduce tensions between the different groups, which in turn can facilitate the smooth completion of the merger or acquisition. Additionally, by being friendly to no one, the management team can avoid forming personal connections that could compromise their ability to make difficult decisions that may be required for the success of the merger or acquisition.

CHAPTER 2: DECIDE TO BE AGGRESSIVE ENOUGH, QUICKLY ENOUGH

"The difference between try and triumph is just a little umph!" - Marvin Phillips

"Decide to be aggressive ENOUGH, quickly ENOUGH" - In business, this means being decisive and taking action when necessary, but also being mindful of not being too aggressive and risking negative consequences.

In the competitive world of business, it is important to be decisive and take action when necessary. However, it is also important to be mindful of not being too aggressive and risking negative consequences. This is where the principle of "Decide to be aggressive ENOUGH, quickly ENOUGH" comes in.

Being aggressive means taking initiative and being proactive in reaching goals and achieving success. It means identifying opportunities and taking advantage of them. It also means being assertive and standing up for what is best for the company or project.

However, being too aggressive can lead to rash decisions and negative consequences. It can also lead to a confrontational relationship with colleagues, clients, and competitors. It's important to find the right balance of aggression and caution.

By following the principle of "Decide to be aggressive ENOUGH, quickly ENOUGH," one can take decisive action while also being mindful of potential consequences. It means taking calculated risks and being aware of the potential downsides.

In addition, being quick in decision making is crucial in today's fast-paced business environment. It means identifying opportunities and taking advantage of them before competitors do. It also means being responsive to changing market conditions and adapting strategies accordingly.

As you can see, this second rule highlights the importance of being assertive and proactive in reaching goals and achieving success, while still being mindful of potential negative consequences and being quick in decision making. This chapter can be extended in much more detail, but I hope this gives you an idea of how the rule can be expanded upon.

Business Rules as they apply to Rule 2:
1. Take initiative: It's important to take initiative and be aggressive in pursuing business opportunities and making decisions.
2. Be decisive: It's important to be decisive and make decisions quickly, rather than procrastinating or hesitating.
3. Be assertive: It's important to be assertive in communication and negotiation, and to stand up for your interests and those of your business.
4. Be proactive: It's important to be proactive in identifying and addressing potential problems or opportunities, rather than waiting for them to come to you.
5. Be opportunistic: It's important to be opportunistic and seize opportunities as they arise, rather than waiting for the perfect opportunity.

Real World Application:

A small startup company is developing a new app that has the potential to disrupt the market. However, the company is facing fierce competition from well-established players in the industry. To succeed, the company needs to be aggressive enough, and quickly enough, to capture market share and attract customers before the competition can respond.

In this scenario, applying rule 2 of being aggressive enough, quickly enough, would involve the startup taking bold steps to promote their app and gain market share as soon as possible. This could include implementing an aggressive marketing campaign, offering discounts to early adopters, or leveraging partnerships to gain access to new customers. Additionally, the startup should be prepared to make quick decisions, such as investing in additional resources or hiring new staff to help scale their operations. By being aggressive enough, and quickly enough, the startup can gain a foothold in the market and establish themselves as a major player in their industry.

CHAPTER 3: HAVE A PLAN

He who fails to plan, plans to fail." - Sir Winston Churchill

"Have a plan" - In business, this means having a clear strategy and goals for the company or project.

In the business world, having a clear strategy and goals for the company or project is crucial for success. This is where the principle of "Have a plan" comes in.

Having a plan means setting clear and specific objectives for the company or project. It also means identifying the steps and resources needed to achieve these objectives. It means having a clear vision of what the end goal looks like and what needs to be done to get there.

A well-crafted plan is a powerful tool to align the efforts of an entire organization towards a common goal, it helps to set priorities, allocate resources, and measure progress. It is also a valuable communication tool that helps to explain the company's direction to stakeholders and employees.

However, a plan is only as good as its execution, it's important to regularly review the plan and adjust it as necessary in response to new information or changing circumstances. A plan that is not executed or reviewed is not much more than an intellectual exercise.

By following the principle of "Have a plan," one can ensure that the company or project has a clear direction and the means to achieve success.

As you can see, this third rule highlights the importance of having a clear strategy and goals for the company or project, and the importance of regularly reviewing and adjusting the plan as necessary.

Business Rules as they apply to Rule 3:
1. Be prepared: It's important to be prepared and have a plan in place for different business scenarios, such as market changes or unexpected events.
2. Set goals: It's important to set clear and measurable goals for your business and develop a plan to achieve them.
3. Prioritize: It's important to prioritize and focus on the most important tasks and goals, and develop a plan to achieve them.
4. Be organized: It's important to be organized and have a plan for how to allocate resources, such as time and money, to achieve your goals.
5. Be flexible: It's important to be flexible and be able to adapt your plan as needed, in response to changing circumstances or new information.

Real World Application

A large corporation is planning to expand its operations into a new market, but is uncertain about how to best approach the venture. The company has a lot of resources, but they need to be used effectively to ensure the success of the expansion.

In this scenario, applying rule 3 of having a plan, would involve the corporation carefully planning and strategizing the expansion. This could include researching the market, identifying potential customers and partners, and developing a clear vision for how the company will operate in the new market. Additionally, the corporation should establish clear goals and objectives for the expansion, and develop a detailed plan outlining the steps needed to achieve these goals. By having a plan in place, the corporation can ensure that its resources are used effectively, and that the expansion is executed in a way that maximizes the chances of success.

CHAPTER 4: HAVE A BACK-UP PLAN

"In every crisis, there is a message. Crises are nature's way of forcing change - breaking down old structures, shaking loose negative habits so that something new and better can take their place." - Susan L. Taylor

Have a back-up plan, because the first one probably won't work - In business, this means having contingency plans in place for when things don't go as expected.

In the unpredictable world of business, it is important to have contingency plans in place for when things don't go as expected. This is where the principle of "Have a back-up plan, because the first one probably won't work" comes in.

A back-up plan means having alternative courses of action ready in case the primary plan doesn't succeed. It means anticipating potential obstacles and having a plan to overcome them. It also means having a plan B, C and D in case of unforeseen circumstances.

Having a back-up plan also means being flexible and adaptable. It means being open to changing course if necessary and being able to pivot quickly when faced with new information or unexpected developments.

It's important to note that a back-up plan is not a sign of failure, it's a sign of foresight and preparation. A back-up plan can be the difference between a crisis and a minor setback.

By following the principle of "Have a back-up plan, because the first one probably won't work," one can ensure that the company or project is prepared for any eventuality and can adapt quickly to changing circumstances.

As you can see, this fourth rule highlights the importance of having alternative courses of action ready in case the primary plan doesn't succeed, and being flexible and adaptable.

Business Rules as they apply to Rule 4:
1. Be ready for the unexpected: It's important to be ready for the unexpected and have a back-up plan in case your primary plan doesn't work out.
2. Be resilient: It's important to be resilient and not let setbacks discourage you, but rather have a back-up plan to move forward.
3. Be proactive: It's important to be proactive and anticipate potential problems and have a back-up plan in place to deal with them.
4. Be adaptable: It's important to be adaptable and able to pivot to a new plan if the original one doesn't work out.
5. Be risk-aware: It's important to be aware of the potential risks associated with a plan and have a back-up plan to mitigate them.

Real World Application:
A business is about to launch a new product, but the launch date is rapidly approaching and there are still some unforeseen issues that need to be addressed.

In this scenario, applying rule 4 of having a back-up plan, because the first one probably won't work, would involve the business being prepared with a plan B in case the initial launch plan doesn't go as smoothly as expected. This could include having a contingency plan in place in case of supply chain disruptions, testing multiple launch strategies, and having a crisis communication plan ready in case of negative feedback.

Additionally, the business should be prepared to adapt and pivot quickly if necessary. By having a back-up plan, the business can minimize the risks of the launch and be ready to act quickly if things don't go as planned.

CHAPTER 5: BE POLITE, BE PROFESSIONAL, BUT HAVE A PLAN

"The only way to win is to have a plan, execute it flawlessly, and be willing to kill anyone who gets in your way." - Mark Cuban

"Be polite. Be professional. But, have a plan to kill everyone you meet." - In business, this means being respectful and professional in all interactions with colleagues, competitors, and clients, but also having a plan for how to outcompete and come out on top.

In the competitive business world, it's important to be respectful and professional in all interactions with colleagues, competitors, and clients. However, it's also important to have a plan for how to outcompete and come out on top. This is where the principle of "Be polite. Be professional. But, have a plan to kill everyone you meet" comes in.

Being polite and professional means being respectful, punctual, attentive and responsive to others' needs, and being honest and transparent in all communications. It also means being courteous and respectful to everyone, including competitors and colleagues. However, it's also important to have a plan for how to outcompete and come out on top. This means being aware of the competition, identifying their strengths and weaknesses and finding ways to gain a competitive advantage. It also means being innovative and finding new ways to improve products or services.

It's important to note that this principle does not suggest being unethical or ruthless, but rather being aware of the competition and having a plan to outcompete them in a legal and ethical way.
By following the principle of "Be polite. Be professional. But, have a plan to kill everyone you meet," one can maintain a respectful and professional demeanor while also being aware of the competition and having a plan to outcompete them.
As you can see, this fifth rule highlights the importance of being respectful, professional and polite in all interactions, while also being aware of the competition and having a plan to outcompete them in a legal and ethical way.

Business Rules as they apply to Rule 5:
1. Maintain professionalism: It's important to maintain a professional demeanor and treat all colleagues, clients and partners with respect, regardless of the level of competition.
2. Build a professional network: It's important to build a professional network and maintain positive relationships with people in your industry, even if you consider them competitors.
3. Be aware of potential threats: It's important to be aware of potential threats, such as competitors, and take steps to protect yourself and your business.
4. Be strategic in your communication: It's important to be strategic in your communication and not reveal too much personal information or share confidential information with the wrong people.
5. Be prepared to compete: It's important to be prepared to compete and have a plan in place to deal with competitive pressure, whether it is by differentiating oneself from the competition or by finding other ways to win.

Real World Application:

A business is going through a merger and acquisition process, and there are concerns about how to maintain good relationships with both the employees of the acquired company and the stakeholders of the acquiring company.

In this scenario, applying rule 5 of being polite, professional but having a plan to kill everyone you meet, would involve the business being strategic in their approach to the merger and acquisition. This could include having a plan in place to effectively communicate the benefits of the merger to both sets of employees and stakeholders, while also being transparent about any potential negative impacts. Additionally, the business should be prepared to address any concerns or resistance that may arise during the process, and be ready to make difficult decisions if necessary. By being polite and professional, the business can maintain positive relationships with all parties involved, while also being prepared to take action if necessary to ensure the success of the merger.

CHAPTER 6: USE THE RIGHT TOOLS

"The right tool for the job is the one that reaches the goal." - Elon Musk

Do not attend a gunfight with a handgun whose caliber does not start with a '4'" - In business, this means being well-prepared and using the best tools and resources available to succeed.

In the business world, being well-prepared and using the best tools and resources available is crucial for success. This is where the principle of "Do not attend a gunfight with a handgun whose caliber does not start with a '4'" comes in.

This principle suggests that in order to succeed, one must use the best tools and resources available. In a business context, this means using the best software, equipment, and resources to increase productivity and efficiency. It also means investing in training and development for employees to ensure they have the skills and knowledge to succeed.

It's important to note that this principle does not suggest using the most expensive or the latest tools, but rather the right tools for the job. It means taking the time to research and choose the best tools and resources to achieve the objectives.

By following the principle of "Do not attend a gunfight with a handgun whose caliber does not start with a '4'," one can ensure that the company or project is well-prepared and using the best tools and resources available to achieve success.

As you can see, this sixth rule highlights the importance of being well-prepared and using the best tools and resources available to achieve success.

Business Rules as they apply to Rule 6:
1. Be prepared: It's important to be prepared and have the necessary tools and resources to deal with any situation.
2. Invest in quality equipment: It's important to invest in quality equipment and resources, and not to skimp on quality in order to save money.
3. Continuously improve: It's important to continuously improve and upgrade equipment and resources as necessary to stay ahead of the competition.
4. Have a backup plan: It's important to have a backup plan and resources in case the primary equipment or resources fail.
5. Be aware of the latest technology: It's important to be aware of the latest technology and advancements in the industry, in order to stay ahead of the competition.

Real World Application:
A business is in the process of developing a new software product and there are concerns about the scalability and performance of the product when it is released to a large number of users.
In this scenario, applying rule 6 of not attending a gunfight with a handgun whose caliber does not start with a "4", would involve the business investing in high-quality and reliable technology, such as using a programming language that is known to be efficient and scalable or using a cloud infrastructure provider that can handle large amount of traffic. By using the best tools and resources available, the business can ensure that their product is able to handle the demands of a large number of users and perform well. This can prevent potential issues like poor performance, scalability problems, and poor user experience, which can damage the reputation of the company and affect the revenue.

CHAPTER 7: INVEST IN YOUR GOALS

"You have to be burning with an idea, or a problem, or a wrong that you want to right. If you're not passionate enough from the start, you'll never stick it out." - Steve Jobs

"Anything worth shooting is worth shooting twice. Ammo is cheap. Life is expensive." - In business, this means being thorough and persistent in pursuing goals and not being afraid to invest resources to achieve success.

In the business world, being thorough and persistent in pursuing goals is crucial for success. This is where the principle of "Anything worth shooting is worth shooting twice. Ammo is cheap. Life is expensive" comes in.

This principle suggests that in order to succeed, one must invest in their goals and not be afraid to spend resources to achieve them. In a business context, this means investing in marketing and advertising, research and development, and employee training. It also means being persistent in pursuing goals and not giving up easily.

It's important to note that this principle does not suggest recklessly spending resources, but rather making strategic investments to achieve success. It means being willing to spend resources to achieve the desired outcome and not being afraid to make mistakes.

By following the principle of "Anything worth shooting is worth shooting twice. Ammo is cheap. Life is expensive," one can ensure that the company or project is investing in its goals and being persistent in achieving success.

As you can see, this seventh rule highlights the importance of investing in your goals and being persistent in achieving success.

Business Rules as they apply to Rule 7:
1. Invest in what is important: It's important to invest in what is important, whether it be a specific product, service, or project.
2. Be efficient: It's important to be efficient in the use of resources and not waste them on things that are not important.
3. Prioritize: It's important to prioritize what is important and allocate resources accordingly.
4. Learn from failure: It's important to learn from failure and not repeat mistakes, but rather invest in what is important
5. Don't be afraid to take calculated risks: It's important to take calculated risks when necessary to invest in what is important, in order to achieve success.

Real World Application

A business is launching a new marketing campaign for a product, but there are concerns about the effectiveness of the campaign and whether it will generate the desired sales results.

In this scenario, applying rule 7 of anything worth shooting is worth shooting twice. Ammo is cheap. Life is expensive, would involve the business being willing to invest in multiple marketing tactics to ensure the campaign's success. This could include using a combination of different advertising channels, such as social media, email marketing, and paid advertising, as well as testing different messaging and targeting strategies. By using a multi-pronged approach and being willing to invest in multiple tactics, the business can increase the chances of the campaign being successful and generating the desired sales results. Additionally, by testing and evaluating the effectiveness of different tactics, the business can optimize their approach and improve their chances of success in the future.

CHAPTER 8: CREATE DISTANCE

"The best competitive advantage is the ability to learn faster than your competition." - Arie de Geus

"Move away from your attacker. Distance is your friend. (Lateral and diagonal movement are preferred)" - In business, this means avoiding confrontations and instead finding ways to outmaneuver competitors.

In the competitive business world, it's important to create distance from competitors and potential threats. This is where the principle of "Move away from your attacker. Distance is your friend. (Lateral and diagonal movement are preferred.)" comes in. This principle suggests that in order to succeed, one must create distance from competitors and potential threats. In a business context, this means diversifying products or services, expanding into new markets, and building strong relationships with suppliers and partners. It also means being aware of potential threats and taking steps to mitigate them.

It's important to note that this principle does not suggest isolationism or avoidance, but rather creating a strategic distance that allows for flexibility and the ability to adapt to changing circumstances.

By following the principle of "Move away from your attacker. Distance is your friend. (Lateral and diagonal movement are preferred.)," one can ensure that the company or project is creating distance from competitors and potential threats, and is positioned for success in the long-term.

As you can see, this eighth rule highlights the importance of creating distance from competitors and potential threats in order to position the company or project for success in the long-term.

Business Rules as they apply to Rule 8:
1. Be adaptable: It's important to be adaptable and be able to change course when necessary, whether it be in response to market changes, new competitors, or other threats.
2. Maintain strategic distance: It's important to maintain strategic distance from the competition, whether it be through diversification or other means.
3. Be aware of potential threats: It's important to be aware of potential threats, such as competitors, and take steps to protect yourself and your business.
4. Diversify: It's important to diversify and not put all your eggs in one basket, in order to mitigate risk and capitalize on new opportunities.
5. Keep perspective: It's important to keep perspective and not get too close to the competition or other potential threats, in order to maintain a strategic advantage.

Real World Application:
A business is facing a crisis due to a negative public opinion about the company or one of its products, which is affecting its reputation and sales.

In this scenario, applying rule 8 of moving away from your attacker. Distance is your friend, would involve the business taking steps to distance themselves from the negative perception and to address the crisis. This could include implementing a public relations strategy to address and mitigate the negative sentiment, such as by issuing a public apology or by taking steps to address the problem that caused the crisis. Additionally, the company should be transparent and communicate clearly and frequently with the public and stakeholders, providing them with the necessary information to understand the situation and the actions taken. By creating distance between the company and the crisis, the business can minimize the damage to its reputation and begin to repair its image.

CHAPTER 9: USE COVER OR CONCEALMENT

"In a rapidly changing business environment, the ability to use cover and concealment to gain a competitive edge is essential." - Mark Zuckerberg

"Use cover or concealment as much as possible" - In business, this means using discretion and tact when handling sensitive information or situations.

In the business world, it's important to protect oneself and one's assets from potential threats. This is where the principle of "Use cover or concealment as much as possible" comes in.

This principle suggests that in order to succeed, one must protect oneself and one's assets from potential threats. In a business context, this means implementing proper security measures, such as firewalls, encryption, and access controls to protect against cyber threats. It also means having proper insurance and backup plans to protect against potential financial losses.

It's important to note that this principle does not suggest being paranoid or excessively secretive, but rather being aware of potential threats and taking steps to mitigate them.

By following the principle of "Use cover or concealment as much as possible," one can ensure that the company or project is protected from potential threats and can continue to operate without interruption.

As you can see, this ninth rule highlights the importance of protecting oneself and one's assets from potential threats by using cover or concealment.

Business Rules as they apply to Rule 9:
1. Protect your intellectual property: It's important to protect your intellectual property and take steps to safeguard your ideas and innovations.
2. Be aware of your competition: It's important to be aware of the competition and take steps to protect your business from them.
3. Be strategic in communication: It's important to be strategic in your communication, and to share information with the right people and keep sensitive information confidential.
4. Be aware of potential threats: It's important to be aware of potential threats and take steps to protect yourself and your business from them.
5. Have a plan for risk management: It's important to have a plan for risk management and to take steps to mitigate risks that could potentially harm your business.

Real World Application:
A business is facing a potential lawsuit from a client who is claiming that the company did not adequately protect their confidential information.

In this scenario, applying rule 9 of using cover or concealment as much as possible, would involve the business taking steps to protect itself from the potential legal action by using legal strategies and tactics to mitigate the risk. This could include reviewing and strengthening its current policies and procedures for protecting confidential information, conducting an internal investigation to determine whether there were any breaches of confidential information, and working with legal counsel to build a defense against the claim. Additionally, the company should take steps to limit any further disclosure of the confidential information and make sure that the staff members are aware of the importance of keeping the information safe. By using legal strategies and tactics, the company can reduce the risk of legal action and minimize the potential damage to its reputation.

CHAPTER 10: FLANK YOUR ADVERSARY

"The best offense is a good defense." - Vince Lombardi

"Flank your adversary when possible. Protect yours." - In business, this means finding ways to gain a strategic advantage over competitors.

In the competitive business world, it's important to have a strategic advantage over competitors. This is where the principle of "Flank your adversary when possible. Protect yours" comes in.

This principle suggests that in order to succeed, one must have a strategic advantage over competitors. In a business context, this means identifying and exploiting weaknesses in the competition, and finding ways to differentiate oneself from competitors. It also means protecting one's own weaknesses and vulnerabilities.

It's important to note that this principle does not suggest being unethical or ruthless, but rather being aware of the competition and finding legal and ethical ways to gain an advantage.

By following the principle of "Flank your adversary when possible. Protect yours," one can ensure that the company or project has a strategic advantage over competitors and is better positioned for success.

As you can see, this tenth rule highlights the importance of having a strategic advantage over competitors by exploiting weaknesses in the competition and protecting one's own weaknesses.

Business Rules as they apply to Rule 10:
1. Be strategic: It's important to be strategic in your business decisions and actions, and to always be thinking about ways to gain an advantage over the competition.
2. Be aware of your competition: It's important to be aware of the competition and take steps to protect your business from them.
3. Diversify: It's important to diversify your products, services, and revenue streams to protect your business from market changes or competitors.
4. Be proactive: It's important to be proactive and anticipate potential problems or opportunities, rather than waiting for them to come to you.
5. Be adaptable: It's important to be adaptable and able to pivot to new strategies or markets if your current approach is not working.

Real World Application:
A business is struggling to gain market share in a highly competitive industry.
In this scenario, applying rule 10 of flanking your adversary when possible, would involve the business finding ways to differentiate itself from its competitors and gain an advantage in the market. This could include conducting market research to identify untapped niches or unmet customer needs, developing new products or services to meet those needs, and rebranding or repositioning the company to better target a specific customer demographic. Additionally, the company could explore partnerships or collaborations with other businesses in order to expand its reach and gain access to new customers. By using a combination of market research, product development and

strategic partnerships, the company can gain a foothold in the market and take advantage of opportunities to grow its market share.

CHAPTER 11: PLAY TO WIN

"If you're not playing to win, you're playing not to lose." - Jack Welch, former CEO of General Electric

"Always cheat; always win. The only unfair fight is the one you lose." - In business, this means finding ways to gain a competitive edge, within the bounds of ethical behavior.
In the business world, it's important to have a winning mindset and always strive for success. This is where the principle of "Always cheat; always win. The only unfair fight is the one you lose" comes in.
This principle suggests that in order to succeed, one must always strive to win and not be afraid to bend the rules if necessary. In a business context, this means finding legal and ethical ways to gain an advantage over competitors, such as finding new and innovative ways to improve products or services. It also means being willing to take risks and think outside the box.
It's important to note that this principle does not suggest being unethical or breaking the law, but rather being creative and resourceful in finding ways to succeed.
By following the principle of "Always cheat; always win. The only unfair fight is the one you lose," one can ensure that the company or project is always striving for success and finding legal and ethical ways to gain an advantage.
As you can see, this eleventh rule highlights the importance

of having a winning mindset and always striving for success by finding legal and ethical ways to gain an advantage over competitors.

Business Rules as they apply to Rule 11:
1. Be competitive: It's important to be competitive and always be looking for ways to gain an advantage over the competition.
2. Always strive for success: It's important to always strive for success and not be afraid to take calculated risks in order to achieve it.
3. Be willing to adapt: It's important to be willing to adapt and change your approach if it is not working.
4. Follow the rules, but also find the loopholes: It's important to follow the rules and regulations of the industry, but also find ways to utilize the loopholes to gain an advantage.
5. Be aware of the competition: It's important to be aware of the competition and take steps to protect your business from them.

Real World Application:
A company is struggling to close deals with potential clients due to aggressive competition from other businesses.
In this scenario, applying rule 11 of always cheating and always winning, would involve the company finding ways to gain an edge in negotiations and outmaneuver its competitors. This could include researching potential clients and learning about their needs and pain points, developing unique selling points and value propositions to differentiate the company from its competitors, and being creative and flexible in structuring deals and finding mutually beneficial solutions. Additionally, the company could explore leveraging its existing relationships and networks to

gain inside knowledge of the clients and their decision making processes. By being strategic, well-informed and creative in negotiations, the company can find ways to close more deals and succeed in a competitive market.

CHAPTER 12: FOCUS ON THE BIG PICTURE

"The best leaders have a high Consideration Factor. They think about their people, they think about the business and they think about the customers." - Ken Blanchard, Author and Management Expert.

"In ten years nobody will remember the details of caliber, stance, or tactics. They will only remember who lived." - In business, this means focusing on long-term success rather than short-term wins.

In the business world, it's important to focus on the long-term and not get bogged down in the details. This is where the principle of "In ten years nobody will remember the details of caliber, stance, or tactics. They will only remember who lived" comes in.

This principle suggests that in order to succeed, one must focus on the big picture and not get bogged down in the details. In a business context, this means setting long-term goals and strategies, and not getting too caught up in short-term fluctuations or minor setbacks. It also means being adaptable and willing to change course if necessary.

It's important to note that this principle does not suggest ignoring the details, but rather keeping the big picture in mind and not getting too caught up in short-term fluctuations or minor setbacks.

By following the principle of "In ten years nobody will remember the details of caliber, stance, or tactics. They will only remember who lived," one can ensure that the company or project is focused on the long-term and is adaptable to changing circumstances.

As you can see, this twelfth rule highlights the importance of focusing on the long-term and not getting bogged down in the details in order to be adaptable and successful in the long run.

Business Rules as they apply to Rule 12:
1. Focus on the long term: It's important to focus on the long term and not just on short-term success.
2. Build a strong reputation: It's important to build a strong reputation and be known for your integrity and reliability.
3. Prioritize sustainability: It's important to prioritize sustainability and ensure that the business can continue to succeed in the long term.
4. Continuously improve: It's important to continuously improve and adapt to changing circumstances and new information.
5. Have a vision: It's important to have a vision for the future and strive to achieve it.

Real World Application

A business owner is considering investing in a new technology or process but is unsure if it will be a success in the long term.

In this scenario, applying rule 12, which states that in ten years nobody will remember the details of caliber, stance, or tactics. They will only remember who lived, would involve the business owner focusing on the long-term outcome rather than getting bogged down by short-term concerns. This means considering the potential long-term benefits of the technology or process, such as increased efficiency and cost savings, rather than worrying about the initial investment or the potential for failure. Additionally, the business owner could research and gather data on similar technologies or processes that have been successful in the past, and use that information to make a more informed decision. By taking a long-term perspective and focusing on the potential for success in the future, the business can make strategic investments that will pay off in the long run.

CHAPTER 13: KEEP THE COMMUNICATION AND ACTION FLOWING

"The single biggest problem with communication is the illusion that it has taken place." - George Bernard Shaw

"If you are not shooting, you should be communicating or reloading." - In business, this means being proactive and productive at all times, whether it's communicating with colleagues or preparing for the next task.
In the business world, it's important to keep the communication and action flowing in order to achieve success. This is where the principle of "If you are not shooting, you should be communicating or reloading" comes in.
This principle suggests that in order to succeed, one must keep the communication and action flowing. In a business context, this means actively communicating with employees, clients, and partners, and keeping everyone informed and up-to-date. It also means keeping the workflow and processes running efficiently, and not letting things stagnate.
It's important to note that this principle does not suggest constant action or constant communication, but rather keeping the communication and action flowing in order to achieve success.
By following the principle of "If you are not shooting, you should be communicating or reloading," one can ensure that the

company or project is keeping the communication and action flowing and is well-positioned for success.

As you can see, this thirteenth rule highlights the importance of keeping the communication and action flowing in order to achieve success.

Business Rules as they apply to Rule 13:
1. Communicate effectively: It's important to communicate effectively with colleagues, clients and partners in order to achieve business goals.
2. Be productive: It's important to be productive and use your time effectively, whether it be by working on a project, communicating with others, or planning for the future.
3. Be proactive: It's important to be proactive and take initiative in your work, rather than waiting for things to happen.
4. Continuously improve: It's important to continuously improve and adapt to changing circumstances and new information.
5. Be organized: It's important to be organized and have a plan for how to allocate resources, such as time and money, to achieve your goals.

Real World Application:
A sales team is struggling to close deals and meet their quarterly goals.

In this scenario, applying rule 13, which states that if you are not shooting, you should be communicating or reloading, would involve the sales team focusing on their communication and follow-up efforts. This means regularly checking in with potential clients, addressing any concerns or objections they may have, and finding new leads to pursue. Additionally, the sales team could review and improve their sales pitch and materials to ensure they are effectively communicating the value of the company's products or services. By focusing on communication and actively pursuing new leads, the sales team can increase their chances of closing deals and meeting their goals. Furthermore, making sure to always have a plan B, or to be ready to reload, will help them to not lose a potential client.

CHAPTER 14: BE PREPARED

"I have always found that plans are useless, but planning is indispensable." - Dwight D. Eisenhower

"Someday someone may kill you with your own gun, but they should have to beat you to death with it because it is empty." - In business, this means being aware of the potential for competitors to imitate or copy your ideas, but always staying ahead and being innovative.

In the business world, it's important to be prepared for any situation. This is where the principle of "Someday someone may kill you with your own gun, but they should have to beat you to death with it because it is empty" comes in.

This principle suggests that in order to succeed, one must be prepared for any situation. In a business context, this means having backup plans and contingencies in place, such as having a disaster recovery plan in case of data loss, or having a plan to deal with unexpected events or market changes. It also means being prepared to adapt to changing circumstances and being able to quickly pivot if necessary.

It's important to note that this principle does not suggest being paranoid or overly cautious, but rather being prepared for any situation and being able to adapt quickly to changing circumstances.

By following the principle of "Someday someone may kill you with your own gun, but they should have to beat you to death with it because it is empty," one can ensure that the company or project is prepared for any situation and is able to adapt quickly to changing circumstances.

As you can see, this fourteenth rule highlights the importance of being prepared for any situation and being able to adapt quickly to changing circumstances in order to be successful.

Business Rules as they apply to Rule 14:
1. Protect your assets: It's important to protect your assets and take steps to safeguard sensitive information and data.
2. Be efficient: It's important to be efficient in the use of resources and not waste them on things that are not important.
3. Continuously improve: It's important to continuously improve and upgrade equipment and resources as necessary to stay ahead of the competition.
4. Have a backup plan: It's important to have a backup plan and resources in case the primary equipment or resources fail.
5. Be aware of the latest technology: It's important to be aware of the latest technology and advancements in the industry, in order to stay ahead of the competition.

Real World Application:
A company's IT department is facing a potential data breach.
In this scenario, applying rule 14, which states that someday someone may kill you with your own gun, but they should have to beat you to death with it because it is empty, would involve the IT department taking proactive measures to prevent a data breach from occurring. This means regularly updating security software and protocols, monitoring for suspicious activity, and implementing strict access controls for sensitive data. Additionally, the IT department could conduct regular

security audits and penetration testing to identify and address any vulnerabilities in the company's systems. By being proactive in their approach to security, the IT department can ensure that even if a data breach does occur, the attacker will not be able to access or steal any sensitive information. Furthermore, if the IT team is well prepared they will be able to respond effectively to any attack and minimize the damage.

CHAPTER 15: MAINTAIN VIGILANCE

"Vigilance is the price of success in the business world, and those who fail to pay it will be left behind." - Richard Branson

"And above all ... don't drop your guard." - In business, this means remaining vigilant and aware of potential threats or opportunities at all times.
In the business world, it's important to maintain vigilance and not let one's guard down. This is where the principle of "And above all ... don't drop your guard" comes in.
This principle suggests that in order to succeed, one must maintain vigilance and not let one's guard down. In a business context, this means being aware of potential threats, such as changes in the market, new competitors, and changes in technology. It also means being proactive in addressing these threats and not becoming complacent.
It's important to note that this principle does not suggest being paranoid or overly cautious, but rather being aware of potential threats and taking proactive steps to address them.
By following the principle of "And above all ... don't drop your guard," one can ensure that the company or project is aware of potential threats and is taking proactive steps to address them, thus positioning the company or project for long-term success.
As you can see, this fifteenth rule highlights the importance of maintaining vigilance and not letting one's guard down in order

to be aware of potential threats and position the company or project for long-term success. This chapter can be extended in much more detail, but I hope this gives you an idea of how the rule can be expanded upon.

Business Rules as they apply to Rule 15:
1. Maintain vigilance: It's important to maintain vigilance and be aware of potential threats, whether they be market changes, new competitors, or other risks.
2. Continuously improve: It's important to continuously improve and adapt to changing circumstances and new information.
3. Be proactive: It's important to be proactive and anticipate potential problems or opportunities, rather than waiting for them to come to you.
4. Have a plan for risk management: It's important to have a plan for risk management and to take steps to mitigate risks that could potentially harm your business.
5. Stay informed: It's important to stay informed about the industry, the competition, and current events in order to be aware of potential threats and opportunities.

Real World Application:
In a rapidly changing market, a company's ability to adapt and stay ahead of the competition is crucial for success. Rule 15, "And above all ... don't drop your guard," is an important principle for businesses to adopt in order to remain competitive.
A real-world scenario where this rule would be applied could be a company that is facing new market entrants and increased competition. In order to stay ahead, the company's leadership team would need to consistently be on the lookout for potential threats, such as new competitors or changes in consumer preferences, and take proactive steps to address them. This could include investing in market research and analysis, staying up-to-date with industry developments and trends, and

continually reevaluating and adjusting the company's strategy and operations. Additionally, the company should have a back-up plan in place in case their primary strategy doesn't succeed, so they can pivot and adapt quickly to changing market conditions. By staying vigilant and not dropping their guard, the company can protect their market position and continue to thrive in the face of competition.

List of Business Principles:

- Maintain professionalism: It's important to maintain a professional demeanor and treat all colleagues, clients and partners with respect, regardless of the level of competition.
- Be aware of potential threats: It's important to be aware of potential threats, such as competitors, and take steps to protect yourself and your business.
- Be strategic in communication: It's important to be strategic in communication and not reveal too much personal information or share confidential information with the wrong people.
- Be decisive: It's important to be decisive and make decisions quickly, rather than procrastinating or hesitating.
- Be proactive: It's important to be proactive and anticipate potential problems or opportunities, rather than waiting for them to come to you.
- Be prepared: It's important to be prepared and have a plan in place for different business scenarios, such as market changes or unexpected events.
- Prioritize: It's important to prioritize and focus on the most important tasks and goals, and develop a plan to achieve them.
- Be organized: It's important to be organized and have a plan for how to allocate resources, such as time and money, to achieve your goals.
- Be adaptable: It's important to be adaptable and able to pivot to new strategies or markets if your current approach is not working.
- Build a professional network: It's important to build a professional network and maintain positive relationships with people in your industry, even if you don't consider them friends.
- Be assertive: It's important to be assertive in communication and negotiation, and to stand up for your interests and those of your business.

- Be opportunistic: It's important to be opportunistic and seize opportunities as they arise, rather than waiting for the perfect opportunity.
- Be ready for the unexpected: It's important to be ready for the unexpected and have a back-up plan in case your primary plan doesn't work out.
- Be resilient: It's important to be resilient and not let setbacks discourage you, but rather

Appendix A. Business Assessment

- Maintain professionalism: It's important to maintain a professional demeanor and treat all colleagues, clients and partners with respect, regardless of the level of competition.
    - How do you currently ensure that all members of your team maintain a professional demeanor in their interactions with colleagues, clients, and partners?
    - How do you handle instances where a team member does not uphold a professional demeanor in their interactions with others?
    - How do you ensure that personal feelings or biases do not influence the decisions or actions of team members in their interactions with colleagues, clients, and partners?
    - How do you measure the level of respect shown by team members towards colleagues, clients, and partners?
    - How do you prepare team members to handle competitive situations and maintain a professional demeanor in those instances?
- Be aware of potential threats: It's important to be aware of potential threats, such as competitors, and take steps to protect yourself and your business.
    - How do we currently monitor and assess potential threats from competitors in our industry?
    - How have we taken steps to protect our business from these potential threats in the past?
    - Are there any areas of our business that we believe to be particularly vulnerable to competitive threats?
    - How do we ensure that all employees are aware of and prepared to deal with potential competitive threats?
    - Are there any areas where we could improve in terms of identifying and addressing potential competitive threats?
- Be strategic in communication: It's important to be

strategic in communication and not reveal too much personal information or share confidential information with the wrong people.
    - How well do you think your company currently protects confidential information and personal information from being shared with the wrong people?
    - What steps does your company take to ensure that communication with clients and partners is strategic and not revealing too much personal information?
    - How does your company evaluate the potential threats from competitors and other external factors?
    - How does your company respond to potential threats and protect itself from them?
    - Are there any past instances where your company's confidential information or personal information was accidentally shared or compromised? If so, what steps were taken to prevent it from happening again?

- Be decisive: It's important to be decisive and make decisions quickly, rather than procrastinating or hesitating.
    - How quickly do we make important decisions within our organization?
    - Are there any common reasons why our decision-making process may become delayed?
    - Are there any individuals or teams within our organization who struggle with being decisive?
    - How do we ensure that all members of our team are comfortable and confident in making quick decisions?
    - Are there any steps that we can take to improve our overall decision-making process and become more decisive as a company?

- Be proactive: It's important to be proactive and anticipate potential problems or opportunities, rather than waiting for them to come to you.
    - How does our company actively seek out potential

threats, such as competitors?
- How do we ensure that personal or confidential information is kept secure in communication?
- Are decisions made quickly and efficiently, or do we tend to procrastinate or hesitate?
- How does our company stay proactive in identifying and addressing potential problems or opportunities?
- Are there any areas in which our company could improve in being proactive and anticipating potential issues?

- Be prepared: It's important to be prepared and have a plan in place for different business scenarios, such as market changes or unexpected events.
  - How often do we review and update our emergency response plan for unexpected events?
  - Do we have a plan in place for how to handle market changes?
  - Have we conducted regular risk assessments to identify potential business scenarios and their impact on our operations?
  - How do we ensure that our employees are prepared to handle unexpected situations?
  - Have we allocated sufficient resources to be able to respond quickly and effectively to unexpected events?

- Prioritize: It's important to prioritize and focus on the most important tasks and goals, and develop a plan to achieve them.
  - How do you determine which tasks and goals are most important for your business?
  - Are there any areas where you feel you are not effectively prioritizing?
  - Are there any specific strategies or tools that you use to prioritize tasks and goals?
  - Are there any areas where you feel like you

are struggling to make progress because you are not effectively prioritizing?
    - Have you ever experienced any negative consequences as a result of not prioritizing effectively? How did you address this problem?
- Be organized: It's important to be organized and have a plan for how to allocate resources, such as time and money, to achieve your goals.
    - Are we effectively prioritizing our tasks and goals?
    - Do we have a clear plan for allocating our resources, such as time and money?
    - Are we regularly reviewing and adapting our plan to ensure we are using our resources efficiently?
    - Do we have systems in place to track our progress and measure our success in achieving our goals?
    - Are we regularly conducting self-evaluations to identify areas for improvement and make necessary adjustments?
- Be adaptable: It's important to be adaptable and able to pivot to new strategies or markets if your current approach is not working.
    - How do we currently handle changes in the market or industry?
    - Are we able to quickly pivot and adjust our strategies as needed?
    - Have we identified potential new markets or opportunities for growth?
    - Are we open to trying new approaches and methods, even if they deviate from our current plan?
    - How do we measure and track our ability to adapt and make changes in our business?
- Build a professional network: It's important to build a professional network and maintain positive relationships with people in your industry, even if you don't consider them

friends.
- How often do we make an effort to network with other professionals in our industry?
- How do we maintain communication and relationships with our professional contacts?
- Are there any specific industry leaders or influencers that we actively try to connect with?
- How do we approach building relationships with competitors in a professional and strategic manner?
- Have we ever leveraged our professional network to gain new business or opportunities?

- Be assertive: It's important to be assertive in communication and negotiation, and to stand up for your interests and those of your business.
  - Are we clearly communicating our needs and wants in negotiations and meetings?
  - Do we take a passive approach in discussions or do we actively advocate for our position?
  - Are we confident in our ability to assert ourselves in difficult situations or with difficult people?
  - Are there instances where we have not stood up for our interests or those of the business?
  - How do we handle pushback or resistance when advocating for our position?

- Be opportunistic: It's important to be opportunistic and seize opportunities as they arise, rather than waiting for the perfect opportunity.
  - How often do we actively seek out new opportunities for our business?
  - How quickly do we act on opportunities when they present themselves?
  - Do we have a system in place for identifying and evaluating potential opportunities?
  - How comfortable are our team members with taking

calculated risks for the sake of seizing an opportunity?
- Have we missed out on any notable opportunities in the past and, if so, why?

- Be ready for the unexpected: It's important to be ready for the unexpected and have a back-up plan in case your primary plan doesn't work out.
    - How do we currently handle unexpected events or changes in the market?
    - Do we have a back-up plan in place in case our primary plan fails?
    - How do we prepare for potential threats or risks to our business?
    - Are we proactive in anticipating and addressing potential problems?
    - How do we ensure that we are always ready for the unexpected and able to adapt to changing circumstances?

- Be resilient: It's important to be resilient and not let setbacks discourage you, but rather accept the new normal and make plans to capitalize on the shifting landscape
    - How well do we handle unexpected events or changes in our industry?
    - How well do we bounce back from setbacks or failures?
    - Do we have a plan in place for when our primary plan doesn't work out?
    - How well do we adapt to new circumstances and make the most of them?
    - Do we have a culture of resilience within our organization?

Appendix B: Summary list of business principles grouped by major themes

Professionalism:
In terms of business acumen, professionalism refers to the ability to conduct oneself in a manner that is appropriate, ethical, and effective in the business world. This includes having a strong understanding of industry-specific knowledge, as well as possessing the skills and abilities needed to succeed in one's role. In addition, professionalism also requires the ability to interact and communicate effectively with others, including colleagues, clients, and partners.

In terms of the list of 15 rules for a gunfight, professionalism can be seen in the emphasis on maintaining a professional demeanor and treating all colleagues, clients, and partners with respect. The list also highlights the importance of being strategic in communication and not revealing too much personal information, which is a key aspect of professionalism in the business world. Additionally, professionalism is also reflected in the need to be prepared, have a plan in place and be decisive, which are all essential traits of a professional in any industry.

- Maintain a professional demeanor
- Treat colleagues, clients and partners with respect
- Maintain objectivity in interactions
- Build a professional network
- Be aware of potential threats and take steps to protect yourself and your business
- Be strategic in communication

Decision Making:
In terms of business acumen, decision making refers to the process of evaluating options and choosing the best course of action to achieve a specific goal or objective. This requires a thorough understanding of the situation, the available options, and their potential outcomes. Effective decision making also requires the ability to analyze information, identify risks and opportunities, and make choices that are in the best interests of

the organization.

In terms of the list of 15 rules for a gunfight, decision making is reflected in the emphasis on being decisive and making decisions quickly, as well as the need to be prepared and have a plan in place. The list also highlights the importance of taking initiative and being aggressive in pursuing business opportunities, which are key aspects of effective decision making in the business world. Additionally, the list emphasizes the need to be adaptable and able to pivot to a new plan if the original one doesn't work out, which is an important aspect of decision making in today's rapidly changing business environment.

- Take initiative
- Be decisive
- Be assertive in communication and negotiation
- Be proactive in identifying and addressing potential problems or opportunities
- Be opportunistic and seize opportunities as they arise

Preparation:

In terms of business acumen, preparation refers to the process of getting ready for a specific task, event, or situation by gathering the necessary information, resources, and tools, as well as developing a plan of action. This includes identifying potential risks and opportunities, and developing a plan to deal with them. Effective preparation also requires the ability to anticipate the needs of the organization, and to be ready to respond to unexpected events.

In terms of the list of 15 rules for a gunfight, preparation is reflected in the emphasis on being prepared and having a plan in place for different business scenarios, such as market changes or unexpected events. The list also highlights the importance of investing in quality equipment, and being ready for the unexpected, which are key aspects of effective preparation in the business world. Additionally, the list emphasizes the importance of having a back-up plan in case the primary plan doesn't work out, which is an important aspect of preparation in today's rapidly changing business environment.

- Be prepared and have a plan in place for different business scenarios
- Set clear and measurable goals for your business
- Prioritize and focus on the most important tasks and goals
- Be organized and have a plan for allocating resources
- Be flexible and adapt your plan as needed
- Be ready for the unexpected and have a back-up plan
- Be resilient and not let setbacks discourage you
- Be adaptable and able to pivot to a new plan if necessary
- Be risk-aware and have a back-up plan to mitigate potential risks
- Be prepared to compete and have a plan in place to deal with competitive pressure
- Invest in quality equipment and resources

Awareness:

In terms of business acumen, awareness refers to the ability to perceive and understand the current situation, as well as the potential future developments. This includes being aware of the internal and external factors that can impact the business, such as competitors, market trends, and industry regulations. Additionally, being aware of one's own strengths and weaknesses, as well as those of the organization, can also be important in making sound business decisions and identifying opportunities.

In terms of the list of 15 rules for a gunfight, awareness is reflected in the emphasis on being aware of potential threats, such as competitors, and taking steps to protect yourself and your business. The list also highlights the importance of using cover and concealment, being aware of the surroundings and potential dangers, and being aware of one's own limitations, which are key aspects of effective awareness in the business world. Additionally, the list emphasizes the importance of being aware of the potential risks associated with a plan, which is an important aspect of awareness in today's rapidly changing business environment.

- Focus on the mission
- Maintain situational awareness
- Be aware of your surroundings
- Be aware of your limitations
- Be aware of your environment
- Be aware of your strengths and weaknesses
- Be aware of your assets and liabilities
- Be aware of your options and opportunities
- Be aware of your risks and threats
- Be aware of your vulnerabilities and strengths
- Be aware of your assets, liabilities, options, opportunities, risks, and threats
- Be aware of your environment and surroundings
- Be aware of your mission and objectives
- Be aware of your limitations and strengths
- Be aware of your options and opportunities
- Be aware of your risks and threats
- Be aware of your vulnerabilities and strengths.

Conclusion

In summary, the 15 rules for a gunfight adapted from the US Marine Corps, provide valuable insights and principles that can be applied to the business world to help professionals to improve their performance and achieve their goals. These rules cover several key areas of business acumen, including professionalism, decision making, preparations, and awareness. In terms of professionalism, the rules emphasize the importance of maintaining a professional demeanor and treating all colleagues, clients and partners with respect, even if you don't agree with them or they are not your friends. Additionally, the rules also encourage building a professional network and maintaining positive relationships with people in your industry. In terms of decision making, the rules emphasize the importance of taking initiative, being aggressive, and making decisions quickly. The rules also emphasize the importance of preparations and being prepared by having a plan in place, investing in quality equipment, and being ready for the unexpected. Additionally, the rules encourage being aware of potential threats, such as competitors, and taking steps to protect yourself and your business. Overall, the list of 15 rules for a gunfight provides valuable insights and principles that can be applied to the business world to help professionals to be more prepared, make better decisions, and achieve their goals.

www.ingramcontent.com/pod-product-compliance
Lightning Source LLC
Chambersburg PA
CBHW050310220526
45465CB00005B/1927